Bathing on the Roof

Tracey Rhys is a freelance writer and editor from South Wales. Her poems, stories and essays have appeared in *Poetry Wales*, *New Welsh Review*, *Planet*, *The High Window*, *Dreich*, *Ink Sweat & Tears* and numerous anthologies. A winner of the Poetry Archive's Now: Wordview competition, her writing has been listed for competitions including the Cinnamon Press Pamphlet Competition, the Poetry Wales Pamphlet Competition and the Cardiff International Poetry Competition. Her pamphlet *Teaching a Bird to Sing* was published in 2016. *Bathing on the Roof* is her first collection.

traceyrhys.com

Praise for *Bathing on the Roof*:

'Rhys has some astonishing turns of phrase that stay in the mind, particularly in the tenderly written first half with its focus on the newborn and the unborn: "Look at the knees ready to walk on the ceiling/a thumb, sewn into a mouth as if it were a tap." Particularly endearing is Flood, the effortlessly stylish protagonist of the second half of the collection who's drawn to "modish hessian" and prone to "making a Severn Bridge of herself" with such panache you can't help but fall in love with this character's voice. Tracey Rhys has the knack of getting so close to the reader there is nothing else for it but to hold on for the ride, which in this book is a watery tour de force through a landscape that becomes blurred under layer after layer of water, forcing the reader to feel a rush of energy as Flood swamps familiar landmarks.' – **Samantha Wynne-Rhydderch**

'*Bathing on the Roof* by Tracey Rhys is an accretion of highly inventive, thrilling, intense poems, which are both visually and textually alive and vivid on the page. Thematically powerful and cleverly linked, these poems lead like many tributaries to become a visceral, swirling sea. The biblical character Bathsheba is the powerful driving force through the first half of the collection – Bathsheba revoiced; Bathsheba many-voiced. The second section is titled *Flood* and the pieces within it absolutely leap from the page with their clever wit and stunning content. This section contains so much writing I was mesmerised by – especially the personification of Flood, and her high-sensory, gorgeously expressed interactions with, and effects upon, the land.

'The legend of Bathsheba made its beginning in water, as does this collection – from the opening poem till the closing one, water connects us to our bodies, our place, our memories, loss, our histories, our experiences, our whole lives. Water also connects us to the fluids inside us that have the potential to create life, to hold life even for a while. Rhys writes her way into and out from the shame and the pain of our bodies, and the changes time and circumstance operate upon them.

'Visceral and unafraid, I have thrilled at reading such naming, as I have found great connection with the poems which hold vital dialogues concerning who touches us, and how this is done. Yet, these poems come to us with such a clever, well-edited balance between the weight of the content and the scale of the poems upon the page – in a poem that occupies half a page, I am left with the feeling that I have been taken to huge places, been offered massive concepts so nimbly and with such skill that I applaud the poet. Each poem is an emotive cry – Rhys' voice is strong and expertly controlled, yet so often calm, contemplative and punctuated with such moments of beauty that I have been one moment swept away upon the tide, and in the next moment, have quieted, and have sighed.' – **Jane Burn**

'Tracey Rhys conjures a myriad of voices, from the everywoman Bathsheba finding somewhere safe to bathe, to Flood, who fears nothing but jugs, sandbags and isolation. These characters capture the power, chaos and vulnerability within us all. Perhaps the most prevalent voice, however, is Rhys' own – considered and astute as she asks, *"Where is the flow if not inside me?"*' – **Mari Ellis Dunning**

Bathing on the Roof

Tracey Rhys

PARTHIAN

Parthian, Cardigan SA43 1ED
www.parthianbooks.com
First published in 2025
© Tracey Rhys 2025
ISBN 978-1-917140-48-5
Editor: Susie Wildsmith
Cover image: 'Bathing on the Roof', 2024, by Tracey Rhys
Cover design by Emily Courdelle
Typeset by Elaine Sharples
Proofread by Imogen Davies
Printed and bound by 4edge Limited, UK
Published with the financial support of the Books Council of Wales
British Library Cataloguing in Publication Data
A cataloguing record for this book is available from the British Library
Printed on FSC accredited paper

For Tim, Morgan and Adam. You're the best.

For my parents. For everything.

And for my dear friends, especially the girls.

CONTENTS

Bathsheba

Flood

Bathsheba

Bathing on the Roof

If your bath is not a safe space –
the suds not quite covering your breasts,
pipes groaning like a foot on the stair –
take yourself to the roof
where morning is ghosting,
your breath a furnace.
Wash with water from the slipware jug:
lip generous, a comfortable handle, plain
but capable body. Run
fingers through your hair
until each strand obeys. Break
those that will not give.
Clean your intimate places.
Your only voyeurs are in the trees,
mists enveloping their perches,
waking with their first songs of the day.
And all the world is sleeping.

Incarnations

I have been slim-hipped,
flat-chested. Full breasted.
Girl. Adult. Swayed the belly
carrying   its   foetus.
Engorged breasts, post-natal
slack. There has been the
month-long bleed as if the
bed were a low-lying field
and I, the irrigation channel.
Poppy heads between legs,
red blooms in snow, acrylic
inks poured onto canvas,
brown mud path, black
gloop on a clean skyline. I
have felt the pain, tug, ache,
twist of a rope around
abdomen. Inside, where the
secrets grow.

Consumed

That night, his weight sunk me.
The moon waxed and waned
beyond the see-saw of his back.

There were petals floating,
his legs made riverbanks
for me to snag in.

The scent of hibiscus lapped
at our thighs. Insects watched—
the whir of their small wings.

We cupped them to water.
Lay, proboscis raised,
soft underbellies exposed

listening for the sounds
of the sea in our shells.

Lightbulb

It was nothing much: a plan in a cul-de-sac.
I laid my palm almost on his heart and said,
Shall I call you about sharing a lift to the airport?

In the driveway, friends said goodbye, kissed air,
brushed lips to cheeks. But I wanted to touch
his coat's open front, the wool beside his skin.

We breathed and breathed. Eyes and words
hung where we left them. The streetlights came
on, blinked off, snapped back again.

Bathsheba in Eden

She will return home, her every indiscretion
simmering to steam. She will be happy with a storm
before sun: thorns overhead and not inside.

The only fruit within – the red wine
staining her teeth. Her little tongue will spit
seeds onto her new white dress.

She will wear her hair as if she's rising
from bed – will not draw a line
around her lids, will not draw a line
around her mouth. She will wear nothing

on her cheeks but down, will remove
the silver cuffs from her wrists,
will not wear perfume.

She will listen for the snapping of twigs
in the tall shade of national parks,
her thighs separate as animals
moving in pairs, ready to run.

It will take more than water to clean this
Uriah and David

but Uriah was only doing his job,
where the cargo ships dock at midnight;
debarking until the last box is grounded.

Crates of food and car parts; shipping
containers creaking with the swing of chains—
a game of noughts and crosses.

He was a mug, of course.
Did your bidding. Waited too long
while you buried your conscience.

You gave the nod and the crane's jib fell,
its sharp hook still pointing to the sky—
clipping his temple.

You dropped too – of course you did
– rolled him over, tilted his chin,
let his throat grow open.

By morning, you were in my bed and he
was gone. Blue lights on the water.
A tar-like bloom on the concrete wharf.

I was sick of...

desire

so I gave you my body.
chastity
so I gave you my body.
solitude
so I gave you my body.
anger
so I gave you my body.
fear
so I gave you my body.
loneliness
so I gave you my body.
myself

so the body left me
and sat in judgment
on the ceiling.

To My Dead Husband

There are days
when I want nothing

but your hands
to thread through me.

To draw my lids
like shutters

on the compass
of your chest.

To lift my knees for you,
dovetail our bodies.

To taste you, like a spice
upon my breath.

First Spell

If we can magic our first bleed into being
then I am guilty of witchcraft. I conjured it
from articles in magazines, whispers
from cousins and sisters who bloomed
on each new moon, the colour of the inside
of the mouth, the shape of a river slipping
into estuaries, flowing into the world
sure and hot. Magicked from words
spoken by clipped school nurses;
the diagrams we brought home
the afternoon we got the talk.
The word in my stomach, rolling
off my lips like an incantation:
period.

A Good Leaf

Her first humiliation is watched by birds, circling
at dusk, their cawing – dots she does not join.

She loves her brother. Abe is fast and lean,
as wild as watercress.

He is with her for the walk through the fields.
Keeps watch while she sits on her heels.

She listens for goats bleating. Dogs barking.
The quiet thud of pots on stoves.

Bathsheba finds herself a good leaf. Wipes.
Her brother is storming the grasses.

He pulls out two scraps of boys
like kittens from a wool pit.

Laughing like capuchins,
they kick until he drops them.

Abe says he *will wring out
their small necks, will visit their fathers.*

She howls with shame until he smiles:
They'll only know you from the bottom down.

I am eager to be clean of this

eager to be clean
of dried blood, soiled clothes,
the clots and mosses
of our sweating bodies.

Their ceaseless chatter:
advice on how to *catch*
before the next new moon.
Positions. Prayers.

This camp,
this makeshift causeway,
the red clay wringing
moisture from soil—

where I, whom they call
barren, carve my own spring—
bleed.

The Butterfly House

i.

Nothing remains in the stomach,
not the fruit or the sap of the tree.

Cannot live. Not for the trilling of hungry blackbirds
or the grabbing at midwives' skirts.

We walk in the shadow of ultrasounds.
Dark womb, white spaces.

Observe the heart's palpitations:
a stunned bird in the hand.

Look at the knees, ready to walk on the ceiling.
A thumb, sewn into a mouth as if it were a tap.

ii.

Were you definitely pregnant?

Two days, I've bled, hoping
it will pass as quietly as it grew.

In the absence of a birth, there is an emptying out.
In the aftermath, there will be landslide.

Here is a pessary to rid you your lost foetus.
Fill up the silver bowl with both your selves.
The artificial light winks.
Somewhere in the clots is the little body.
In the flush is the disappearing hope.

In the beginning was the child and the child was lost
and the loss tore open.

Wide wound. Sea breaker.
Neck-high tide.

iii.

Grief must be worn like this.
Buckled up. Just so.

I return to a life but cannot do its job.
I lie in bed and feel dead,

as heavy as topsoil.
Forgive me the weight of the world.

When the third pregnancy comes
and stays

I know what blessing is.
It is *hyperemesis gravidarum.*

Feet kicking. The flipping of butterflies
in the house of an abdomen.

She swung in and out, but they hadn't lost her yet

Slippery island of a bed. Too flat, too high.
Too little use of gravity. She shifted
and the Earth emptied.

Knees planting their tubers,
hips spread into valleys,
mouth a tulip.

Wordless, the pain: a soundscape
of vowels, before the lava is born.
The fight of a lifetime.

First, the head with its unspeakable
agonies. Next, the body,
the bullet shoulders.

The rest is all easy: a lambing.
Throat cleared and bawling,
insects walking wings up the walls.

Straw Dolly

The seamstress, her needles plucked
from a leather wallet, comes to sew me up.

Mouth and nose, eyes and legs,
perineum – flower name.

She makes me to the pattern of a paper rose,
origami for the bedridden, lays a cloth over my knees

as if dressing the table, wipes blood from my lips
as kindly as my own mother.

She makes an eyelet of ripped edges. Good dollies
won't complain at the grind of glass as babe takes teat,

sucks buttons through buttonholes, eyes swimming
in their bluish whites, undoing blanket stitch.

Keeping Pace

Never much of a sprinter until the year the baby was born,
circumnavigating the passers-by, moon-roving out of the semis.
So much feedback from the feet, like old-screen interference
(white noise for the soles). I raced to playgroup. Always late
for the early start, dates with friends, mother and baby classes.
The pushchair wild (too much town for its axles, too many legs
to pick up speed beside the pavement cafes).

I wore unsuitable footwear – boots that made me slow,
sandals that slapped rhythms through the streets. The heels
that let me spy through picture bays. Late for feeds, late for naps,
late for my love come home for evening tea. Sprinting
in my blue jeans, nursing bra, cottonwool soaking up the milk.
Pram wheels whirring to the baby's screams. Always in a state
of flux. Nagging the pavement cracks   to   stop.

Eating the Stars for Supper

He is eating the stars for supper from a cereal box
in which hoops are rings haloing gas giants,
black holes slip to infinity on the underside of the pack.
Palms to the sky, he traces Cassiopeia,
the nose of the butterfly in the double-link of his thumbs.
I wash bowls with full circles, the sponge dull
against porcelain, the cloth licking at ceramic rims.
Lead him to bed with tales of Vega, second brightest
in the northern sky. Draw his curtains as the plastic stars
ignite; their phosphorescence minty as his bedtime breath.
Up above the world so high – *the sky, the sky* –
diamond-cut glasses drain on the plate rack,
each light blazing; a split of the atom.

He tells me how trees communicate

calls it the *Wood Wide Web*. Roots threading
with fungi; the modem of trees.
Code for another way of living.

In droughts like this, tap roots reach
for water, look to trees with deep longing,
wringing out secret reservoirs.

I unravel too, with the sun at its extreme. The air
unreachable. The ground a fractured shell.
I reach out a hand

                              and he takes it,
now beyond the age for embarrassment
at his mother's shows of affection.

The trees speak of it. Ash to ash.
Arteries in their root embrace.

Bathsheba on the Streets

She is as intimate with the rain
as your car window.

She slaps her cheek to the pavement
and it cuffs her back, lies in filth

as machines sweep gutters, waits
in doorways where there is no passage,

wakes on roundabout islands
sharked by commuters.

*

Soon, she will speak to ankles,
recite to heels. Their footprints

on pavements – a braille
for the desperate.

Any spare change please?

Which used to mean *help*
but now means *give me oblivion*

like the girls
in the room at the top.

Women as Negative Space

Woman (1): two-thirds of an armchair,
including the legs. Triangle pockets hang
at her hips. Neck and shoulders:

a bottle of craft ale. The bar splinters
for her talking finger, pointed at: Woman (2)
compromising a loveseat. Light bends

on her cheeks like an angle grinder.
Woman (2): a shadow's frown. The wall grows
arounds her as she shrinks. The stool makes room
but she slips it.

Passes tables crouching with men.
Brass taps spliced with girls.
A mirror shocks her: the detail of strangers.

The door slices open, just a whisker.

Bathsheba in Beverly Hills

Before the cancer took hold, she swore
by the health boon of honey – the finest manuka,
the colour of the skin she'd oiled
at poolside parties in her youth.

When the sun was too hot to escape,
she lay on the frills of her daybed,
dreamt of the stores in Beverly Hills,
dinners at Brentwood, nights

at the Malibu beach house. She recalled
bellhops with their cotton gloves,
their smell in her penthouse, the elevator
carpeted, the rattle as the gates slid shut.

At a dance when she was seventeen,
some stranger in the crowd slid his hand
between her legs, stroked at her vulva,
creased up her new silk dress.

She spun around, expecting –
not those society men, their hair slicked back
like lips, the crystal in their hands,
the way their conversation never
                                        slipped.

Burning the Furniture

This was how he broke his women.
First, he took an axe to their hair,
sliced out their knots.
Next, he splintered their feet,
set them apart. Finally,
he used their own wood to batten
down the hatches. There's no escape
when the door is nailed to your back.
When your palms are tacked to your mouth.
When the dovetail joints have flown.
Only then did he hold her close,
nestle her in the kindling of his arms.
Swan matches smouldering in a pocket.

Bathsheba at the Chapel

Bathsheba is in a hallway,
lit like a Dutch master,
her brown suit slack on her hips,
prayer book in hand.

Here are the faces she no longer sees:
boys from her school, men at the Embassy
Ballroom, the farm hands who drank
with her father, who carried the *Mari Lwyd*.

Chapel, Sundays, she sits with the neighbours,
sings at the stained-glass windows.
They hold their prayer books in one hand, pinch
at the bridge of their noses to pray.

The vicar preaches from Samuel. Wars again.
He won't get off them. Prophets. Kings.
A tune from Vivaldi. *Amen*, they say.
Amen, she mouths.

She can't look at the women,
knows their watery eyes,
the marble of their smiles:
mirrors to her own.

Little Flickers

We never dreamt
ourselves old
in any life.
Ageing yes, but not
this slackening skin,
the hooding of our eyes,
our ebonies blanched
to whites. Our
technicolour hearts
still raging
in the monochrome.

Bathsheba's Relics

After she'd died, they opened the wardrobe.
Carved into the oak was a pelican,
its neck bulging with secrets.

Inside, her perfume hung
on collars and cuffs, their buttonholes
the exact shape of her mouth, its little '*Oh?*'

Amongst the winter coats, they found her
stick. The black one with the brass, its bunch
of grapes that bit into the skin.

For weeks, a prankster woke before the house,
swaggered downstairs in onyx and pearls, tapping
on tiles and varnished boards. How their stomachs

lurched to hear them pass! The familiar groan
of footfall on the bottom stair,
the solid tip of metal on terrazzo floor.

Perennial

You want to watch the bluebells,
they'll take over the beds...

And true enough, by tonight,
you won't see your toes if you stand
in this black soil, blue as the sky after rain.

The cat picks her way between dead heads,
blown by the breeze into bushes.
I pick them up and lay them down,
like books I can't face reading.

When the family comes, they'll shake
out bags with green gloves, snip
stems with secateurs.

This is the garden, they will say,
full and neat and square.

X

Someone is burning letters
    but I can't wait to—
cursives are settling on thorns and nettles
like an early snow
    simply   *the cat*
my neighbour is sorting his bills from his darlings
    you weren't always
edges aflame, they touch down
    Mum   *second*
like the tube dying in an old TV
an afterglow from the deep past
    divided
the air above us blackened
though these fragments keep coming
    has   *divorced*   *nice*
Amongst sycamore seeds
that have spun to a stop.
    civil
In the garden, I bend
to find some wisdom for my life.
Close both eyes. Hold out a palm.
I'll take it as a kiss – those two lines
crossed. The letter x.

Deep Dive

Somewhere in the city we open
windows, lean on the edges
as if checking for rain, reach
out our hands—willows
for water.
Diving bells
for the bottom
of the world.

Diving bells for the bottom
of the world in the traffic,
blasting our horns,
slamming car doors.
We rise up on bridges,
a midnight of pendulums—
strike for the hour
of the world.

We strike for the hour
of the world in our offices.
White-knuckle meetings
in buildings of glass.
Ascend in the lifts—
caged birds in an aviary,
winged on the top
of the world.

We are winged on the top
of the world in our homes
where we draw up our feet

and we shutter the blinds.
Switch on our screens
for the charms of the static:
drift through the words
of the world.

Enter the Water

Tired as an apple tree tethered
to a brick wall, she shucks
the weight of the bedding.
At the top of the house,
in the room with the slanted
ceiling, pigeons and rainclouds above,
two storeys of furniture below,
she enters the water.

There are goosebumps prickling her shoulders.
Her knees are the gnarls of a trunk.
Lines vein her palms like leaves.
Hair is a crown canopy. Why stop
at being a goddess when you can
take off your clothes and root
like a spring cutting? Chill
in the morning gloam and bud.

Flood

Prologue

This flood has turned my world
into a single room. Left me high
and tearful – all my waters gathering.

I see you, old pony on a scrap of land.
The dying light drifts in pools
around your flanks. That cry

of yours: anything might respond:
beaks and teeth, claws and wings,
the water gods, and other things.

Flood

Flood woke up on the wrong side of her bed, flowed over the bank with displeasure. There was power in her upsurge, the great swell of her being. Birds who waded in – the egrets and cormorants – recalled that once Flood was happy, but now was better. By better they meant Ocean. Flood was broad and tidal estuary. She left a salty ring around their beaks and gave them shells. Flood was beautiful, they said. She should stop and feel it. But how could Flood pause when she was all reflection? Moon-driven, surging out to sea.

*

Flood recalled her first taste of tarmac. Compared it to fennel. Preferred it to liquorice. She drawled, No need for glass when you have fibreglass. Or slate stacks, when you have those aching aluminium greys: the skeletons of automobiles. Ever since she'd drunk her first bollard, Flood had regretted concrete. The way it sunk into her pit and stayed there, trolley-bound for years.

*

Stories began circulating that Flood had been a stream, had thought big and got lucky. She was fast becoming folklore. It was true that she'd tried all the tricks; consuming lakes, spouting dams. *I am braver than I know*, Flood told the starlings. *Bigger than is necessary*. Beaks rippled in. The sun gave her prisms. Soon, she was run through with flowing, even as she was imbibed. *I am always inside other bodies*, she confided to the water rats on the underside of her skin.

Interview with a Celebrity

Flood, thanks for taking time out from your urban tour ... I appreciate you must be busy.

Well, I'm nothing without my fans.

And your fans love you.

Why, thank you.

They want me to ask what your favourite colour is.

My favourite colour is calcite. Pearly, like the inside of a tooth, all pulp and tusk. It reminds me of better days; snow quartz skies, rain on the way, white horses rising to pummel the hard brick houses.

Where do you go on holiday?

The fat berg.

Everyone will be surprised by that! I think we imagined the Maldives ...

The fat berg is an island destination, a busman's holiday if you like. Not everyone's choice but I confess to enjoy oozing up through a drain grille, along waste pipes to vanity units, coating myself slick on the gunge loaded with hair in the trap.

What keeps you going?

It has to be the Blob Fish. Have you seen how ugly they look, dead on land? That nose! Almost human. Four thousand feet under the sea they don't look half bad. I live by that.

What are you afraid of?

Jugs.

What advice have you got for our youngsters, starting out?

Get yourself a spot, it doesn't have to be nice. Grow into it. To be small is no small thing. I always felt as big as I could be. As if the air was with me, walls parting at the dam.

Launch Party

She arrived with an entourage.

First was her agent, flashing his emerald fins.
                    Second were the hangers-on,
          striding pink flamingo
                under a disco ball.
                          Trees, flat on their backs,
              spread out their leaves
    to let her walk on them.
Even lightning put in an appearance –
                    a sucker for pyrotechnics.
                          I adore the latest trends,
          she gushed for the magazines,
                pouting at a fish-eye lens.
                          How did it begin? they cooed.
    Had there been a turning point?
          There was a fork in the river,
    she told them. *Yes.*
That peak of the tide.

Cumulonimbus

Flood softened the ceilings that year,
yellowed a patch in the corner of a room,
undetectable until her dripping pocked the night,

a crowd-surf into a bucket of old friends.
In the morning, ceremonially as slops,
they'd throw her out; let her soak

into the lane, its ryegrass eager to seed.
There would be a dry season.
The sort that picks the ground

into open doorways, that parts the soil
until it mimics the lips
of the starving animal.

Things happen when the land is ready.
A symmetry collecting its parts.
In the soil, before those first rains,

she had considered herself dead.
What am I? she wondered.
Where is the flow if not inside me?

Then the sky came to save her,
with all its deluge indignations.
Where would she be without the heroics of clouds?

Flood believes

in wildflowers in feet in the language of fishes in light
in dark in rough tongues and beaks in drowning
and crop circles in dry seasons and jugs in ice
and sewers and bridges and waders and hulls
in absorbent pads in tampons and buoyancy aids
in nighttime and sunshine in shopping trolleys and voices
in drowned rats and sinking claws and rotten planks
in buckets in ladles in kettles in swimming in thirst
in death in height in trees in shadows and paws
in dark green roots thrown deep and low

Playtime

Flood praised the pebbles
for their lightness of touch,
how they skittered
at the fork in her bend
like splinters at the axe.

She played at being the wind,
hurrying downstream
in oceanic ripples.
At a gate, she stopped
to make a game of sinking a bike.

First the tyres
in her brown pit,
then the spokes
sinking cartwheels
into gravel gums.

She was making a Severn Bridge
of herself, all cable-stays
and pannier, crossbar
and D-lock. At the submersible
pump, she said her prayers:

Here lies the end of days.
Prayed like someone at
the grave of past experience:
*May they empty my waters
into my waters.*

New Clothes

That year brought rain in curtains, steel pelmets of flounce,
rivers weaving outrageous tapestries. The sound of them
as they travelled: a chiffon of watercourses. Flood loved it
when the backs burst off wardrobes, bringing pleats
to her double hems, a percussion of tinnitus to her orchestra.

Look how she dresses in the latest detritus! Backs of phones,
roof tiles, empty crisp packets, photographs washed clean
of faces – as if they were old friends:
Ah, paper, weren't you a tree I once knew?
Oh! but plastic, remember the oil fields in my beds.

Home Game

Match in play, Flood rushed the pitch
and saw a body lifted above heads.
> *Dead or wooden?*

Flood saw the home crowd off,
drowned the grass stripes – white lines
milky in the shallows, cream washed from the carton.

She made an island of the goal post, turning
their footprints to mulch. Lager cans bobbed
against advertising hoardings.

In the car park, the away-team
managed to start the bus,
parted her waves like the red sea.

She dampened the spark plugs,
silenced the engine; filled the wing mirrors
with flashbacks of their crash-test dummies.

God, but she was wild that year!

Arrived like an uninvited guest
at a lover's wedding,
an invasive seed on the wind.

She donned pelts like the fevered rich
of the roaring twenties: limp-necked
foxes tumbled upstream.

She made shards of the hot houses.
Splintered their roof tiles, dragged their fences
back to the goods yards.

By day, dogs swam like seals
in her bone and marrow. Their slick
backs were sirens on rocks.

All night, fossil-still in the government palaces,
she blew their electrics. Demonstrated
the art of seeping through locks.

A ripple of glass ruins

If Flood had a vice, it was sand.
Delicious in its boxy bags—
its modish hessian, the stitches
that would hold until they failed.
Sand absorbed her
like sonar in a steel drum,
all whale song and submersibles,
until Flood filled up the dreams
of sand, or sand ran through the dreams
of Flood: women wading out to sea,
men crumbling on waterfronts,
cars and ships carried in a flash mob.
The world above and below the tideline
magnificent in its symmetry.

Out of her Element

Late for the party, a swell of debris for a dress,
hair a copper coil freshly sunk in the docks.

It's so nice to be treated like a regular act of God,
she told an oil drum that had listened for an hour.

The barrel whistled through its cavities, enquired
if she'd like to get some air. Neon lights

whitewashed her surface, danced through her plastic shards
like electric eels.

He was no good, she decided when he asked for a ride on the first date.
She bobbed him like an apple, left him in bits.

Interview with an Act of God

Flood, it's great to see you again. I've got a bucket-load of questions. First, the one that's on everyone's lips – what can we do to avoid you?

Stand on the roofs of your houses. Learn to walk on stilts. Climb uphill. Enjoy the island life. Drink often (boil first). Swim in good saltwater. Build homes like the early shore-dwellers of Scottish lochs – wooden shacks raised on platforms sunk in sub-soil, traps suspended early in the mornings, baskets woven with some trees I used to know.

How long will this continue?

I still feel like the newest thing but really, I'm a comeback kid. Everyone remembers the last time they saw me, drunk and weeping on the roof of a taxi, but never the rising dampness.

What should we do?

Nothing. You have a good seat, my friends. Some are sipping coffees at the edges of desks, miles high in the city. Others have the ground to lose.

What will become of us?

In the future, when you've reverted to type, slipped back to your basest instincts, your animal ancestors will discover the sewers. There will be tangles of you: endless miscellanea. The future is full of it. I wash them without intent, like thoughts sifting through the dying brain. When all is gone, these will remain: steel toecaps, the plastic 'Y' of flip flops, the alphabet of soles: your brands ossified mid-tread.

The Mud Service

So, this is us, a little corner of the fat land,
still talking in our zombie tongue,
still clinging to the accents that they can't decode
unless we pare them down, dampen the consonants,
sharpen the vowels. We are landfill,
and Britannia puts whisky in our evening feed,
lies us down in our bed, face down on the mattress
though she knows she shouldn't chance it,
our drowsiness unnatural, our breathing silent.

Puts camouflage on her dry cheeks,
dresses in secrets; the one with the zip-through middle
she keeps for business. She says,
Always be prepared to turn tricks for the sailors.
They will put their dirty hands on you, in you,
they will stuff you full of Sovereigns.
Let them empty themselves in your depths.
Open up, good girl.
Old girl, who never grows old.

The year the mud was scraped and sunk,
phosphorescence illuminated the coast.
It said, *Look for the boat with the split lip*
dropping its load in the darkness,
lighting the way from Hinkley Point to Penarth Head,
then home to a power-station breakfast.
And we swam in its wisdom.
Soundlessly. Wordlessly.
The beds beneath us shifting.
Bad mother.
Bad mother.
Bad mother.

51

Flashback

1995

Sludge is the new black,
all the young rivulets are wearing it,
Flood runs herself slick through gutters,
scoots along sewers, loosens a drainpipe,
coats herself with gelatinous shit.
Takes everything life offers, for good
or worse. She is a hedonist, oh yes.
But then, aren't all the young?

2025

Flood can't believe that was her.
Too green to know better,
slithering beneath floorboards,
ladled out and flung with sanitary towels,
bucketed into gutters.

She unpicks her history with a kiss-and-tell
journalist. Can hardly recall the night
they are dissecting. Some recollection
of a house beneath hills. Riding

the garden with neat sewage,
carousing over bricks, wending
her way home in the wee hours.
Never the walk of shame for Flood.
Always, the promenade.

Flame Thrower

When they went electric,
Man stopped worshipping Sun.
When they saw its core of gold,
they realised its flaw:
A one-pot chimney:
sinking,
rising,
flame-thrower.
Quite right too.
Fire is the thing
Flood's least afraid of.
All steam and fag-ends,
dying taper in a teacup.
The way Sun
muscles in
on a good downpour
still annoys her.
Its incorrigible beauty
on a blue-black day,
its rainbow hard to ignore.
Exhibitionist flares. Solar storms.
Its awful eclipse!
Hiding behind the skirts
of the moon.

Tryweryn, 1965

A prayer for the animals soon to float;
no more than driftwood, far less than kidskin.
Equal to the tyre kill spread *bara menyn*
under the last bus.

In the grass, a game of Cowboys and Indians:
fingers snapping for guns, stalks under chins,
shirts rising over an ants' nest.

Now, a prayer for the potholes on the bridge.
They shall fill first. Then the kitchen lean-tos
with their fibreglass waves.

The last to go will be the road in;
a beaching of tarmacadam
in this town of drownings.

Years to come, there will be droughts.
Drones will soar over the pickings like doves.

Shame

Though she's old enough to have forgotten
all the embarrassing beginnings,
Flood lets them in at night –
the wind rushing at her edges,
the riverbank audible
in its silver spoons.

Flood remembers her great
shames, burns with them.
Her vast stupidities –
how she once boasted
to the moon that
she had the bigger tides.

She pours herself into
the soft rugs, spreads herself
thinner than vapour – nothing
will find her until morning, when
the tinny glug of her belly
will answer the flushing loos.

Would Rather Be

i.

In reflective moments, Flood
watches birds rising
like sand over dunes.
Their muted wings
gliding
and swooping,
the tips
of their feathers close enough
to wet the oil-slick quill of her.
If Flood could fly,
silver scales at flux
in the bloodstream,
as slippery as them,
lungs beating between palms,
she would flip from her skin
to catch the light.

ii.

When summer comes
with its cracked walnut of a riverbed,
its long veins of dry endings,
Flood wants
to butterfly herself into bluebells. Their heads,
pretty as octopi, stems tinting to violets.

She wants what they rave about at sea:
undulating leaves, stubby saltmarshes,
the woods rooted. Each tentacle
an irrigation channel, and the silt
tumbling into smashed china,
a cabinet of ancestors.

iii.

           Maybe
        next year
      Flood could be
    reborn as Otter?
  All the world loves
him,
cool in his river of $^{light.}$
Fur slicked,
  sky floating.
   The dry world
     falling in ^{seeds}
       on his pelt.
        Oh, for the nut $^{of\ a\ body.}$

Sea Change

I can get there in a season of green shoots.
In short winters and brittle nestings.
In sun-doused summers,
offspring quick to fly.

In autumns that come earlier
every year, leaves flaming
to a standstill. I can take
the slow form of droplets
on your glass, peering
through a lens without a cornea.

I can see your dry sofa interiors, dust
floating in the light shards of your lungs.
I can see you don't need me
but I see you. I'll be there soon.

Notes

The Mud Service: Written in response to the Hinkley Point/Cardiff Bay nuclear mud-dumping scandal of 2018, when the dredging of 320,000 tonnes of mud sediment from outside the new Hinkley C nuclear power station was deposited in the sea at Cardiff Bay. There were fears that the mud could have been contaminated with weapons-grade plutonium from the 1960s, but the Welsh government at the time dismissed the claims in the face of extensive opposition.

Tryweryn: This poem refers to the village of Capel Celyn in North Wales, which was forcibly evacuated and flooded under a Parliamentary Bill in the early 1960s, to provide drinking water for the city of Liverpool. The Welsh phrase in the poem '*bara menyn*' translates to 'bread and butter', referring to being flattened and thinly spread.

Bathsheba and David

The character Bathsheba can be found in the books of 2 Samuel 11-12 and 1 Kings 1-2 in the Old Testament. Originally the wife of Uriah the Hittite, a minor soldier in the army of King David, Bathsheba later became the wife of David and the mother of Solomon, who would inherit the throne. The story goes that the married Bathsheba was undergoing her ritual purification bath after menstruation when she was seen by the king who was stood on a rooftop. He enquired who she was, sent his servants to collect her, and brought her to the palace where they slept together.

A short time later, Bathsheba sent word to the king that she was pregnant. To cover up the adultery, David sent for her husband, Uriah, who was fighting with David's army at Rabbah. Under the guise that he wanted to learn how the battle was progressing, David planned to indulge Uriah, then send him home to sleep with his wife, solving the question of the child's parentage. But Uriah, in his loyalty, refused to leave the palace for the night, instead sleeping alongside the king's servants.

With the plan thwarted, David sent Uriah back to Rabbah with a letter containing orders for his own demise. Joab, the military commander, received a command to position Uriah in an indefensible location in battle, ensuring his death.

With Uriah dead, David was free to take Bathsheba as one of his wives, but their newborn son would later die in its infancy: an outcome which was attributed to divine retribution for David's mortal sins. Bathsheba and David would go on to have another son, Solomon. When she reappears again, in 1 Kings 1-2, she is a much more powerful matriarch, ensuring that her son inherits the throne over his older sibling by subtly reminding David of his earlier promises to her.

A Note about Bathsheba

I first read the story of David and Bathsheba when I was studying for my A level Religious Studies class back in 1990-2. Even as a seventeen-year-old in a pretty sexist era, I could see that there was a basic question about consent here – *was this rape?* I could piece together a case from the spare depiction in the text, or I could leave it to my imagination to guess what that turn of events might have felt like for her – or how I might feel in that position – but we can never really know. Many of the women in the Bible are absent in mind, rather than body. They are the sisters of, mothers of, daughters of, wives of. Bathsheba herself has more lineage than the average woman in the Old Testament because she directly impacts the fates of two major kings (David and Solomon).

What started me writing about Bathsheba, almost thirty years ago, was that one night I went to bed in my back bedroom in my parents' house up in the Rhondda, and I had a vivid dream. I was a grown woman, escaping in the dead of night, with a child. When we arrived at our rendezvous – it was dark, dusty, I was terrified of the lights I could see in a compound in the distance – a group was waiting to take the child from me. I thought we would both be saved, but I was startled when they took the boy from me then whispered, urgently: 'Bathsheba! Bathsheba, go back'.

When I awoke the next morning, my mother began telling me about a vivid dream she'd had the night before. 'Who's Bathsheba?' she said. 'Someone from the Bible, isn't it?' What the hell? We'd had the same dream. Or as near as heck it. Or maybe we didn't, but we were determined to make it so; that's bonds for you. Either way, I took it with me, this dream, and I never forgot it.

So, these poems use Bathsheba's story as a jumping-off point; but to me, Bathsheba is a by-word for anonymity. Every woman whose testimony has been glossed over; whose life's outcome has been decided by others; cherished lovers; abused wives – the lucky ones who escaped, like my father's vivacious late mother, and those who didn't; those who have loved and lost; those who are wonderfully complicated and devastatingly conflicted; the grief-stricken; the physical; the spiritual; the tormented; those who have been casually sexually assaulted – in a pub, a club, walking down the road, in a job, in a classroom, at the house of a friend; those who revel in their own bodies; those who know their own power. This is a little book of poems for you. I should have finished them long ago, but I was too busy doing the chores.

Acknowledgements

Thanks are due to the editors of the following publications, in whose pages some of these poems have previously appeared: Jonathan Edwards and Zoë Brigley at *Poetry Wales*; Emily Blewitt at *New Welsh Review*; Emily Trehair at *Planet: The Welsh Internationalist*; John Lavin at *The Lonely Crowd*; Mark Antony Owen at *Iambapoet*; Mike Jenkins at *Culture Matters*; Jack Caradoc at *Dreich*; David Cooke at *The High Window*; Rebecca Bilkau and Gillian Lambert at *Dragon/Yaffle*. Thanks to David Morley for his online workshop, organised by *Poetry Wales*, in which one of these poems was hatched.

To poets Rhian Edwards, Emily Cotterill, Amanda Rackstraw, Emily Blewitt, Julie Griffiths and Marcelle Farr – my first readers always. You make me a better writer, a deeper thinker, and a louder laugher.

To Beverley Roberts, in honour of the two girls we once were, sitting on the swings up the Darren, talking about becoming writers. We did it.

To my boys, Morgan and Adam, and my husband, Tim Rhys: you make me glad, every day, that whenever I found a four-leaf clover as a child, I wished for love.

For Frances and Michael Davies, for buying me *The Golden Treasury of Poetry* back in 1984 – I've still got it, it set my imagination alight. And for your dedication to the cause of parenting. Without your love, the world would have been a different place.

To Richard Davies and the good people at Parthian, for taking a punt on a middle-aged newbie and making this book a reality; I am more grateful than you could know.

And lastly, to my editor, Susie Wildsmith, for your expertise, insight and support throughout the creative journey; not to mention your friendship – thank you, thank you, thank you.

PARTHIAN *Poetry*

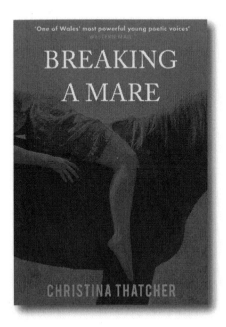

Breaking a Mare
Christina Thatcher
ISBN 978-1-917140-24-9
£10.00 | Paperback

'One of Wales' most powerful young poetic voices.'
– **Jenny White,** *Western Mail*

Breaking a Mare is an investigation of silence, goodness and girlhood. It invites readers into the barn, the sawdust mill, the rodeo arena. These poems expose the hard work women do on farms, the loss of rural landscapes and the role death can play in these spaces. They ask what it means to be good in the face of physical, emotional and ecological threat. Ultimately, these poems want to know what breaks us and what makes us stronger.

Hymnal
Julia Bell
ISBN 978-1-914595-11-0
£10.00 | Paperback

'Moving, tender writing with a haunting evocation of place and time.'
– **Hannah Lowe**

This unique memoir in verse offers a series of snapshots about religion and sexuality. In verse because it's how Bell remembers: snapshots in words strung along a line, which somehow constitute a life. Snapshots of another time from now, but from a time which tells us about how Bell got here. Not the whole story, but her story. Of an English family on a mission from God, of signs and wonders in the Welsh countryside, of difference, and of faith and its loss.

PARTHIAN *Poetry*

Little Universe
Natalie Ann Holborow
ISBN 978-1-917140-21-8
£10.00 | Paperback

'This is intimate, poignant writing. Stunning imagery bursts from these pages as the speaker's selves open to their surroundings, the reader joining a chorus of "startled applause".'
– John McCullough

Lives bustle within a busy hospital's walls, humming against the Gower landscape that stretches beyond its windows. The tiny worlds of a wide cast unfold as they deal with their own emergencies, losses, recoveries, hopes and histories.

This Common Uncommon
Rae Howells
ISBN 978-1-914595-90-5
£10.00 | Paperback

'Finely wrought, intelligent, and full of heart... an important book that speaks for nature, land, and species which, too often, we see as silent: a vital tome at a time of urgency.'
– Mab Jones, *Buzz Magazine*

When a local common is threatened with development, one poet explores its secrets, discovering extraordinary natural treasures and wonderful people fighting to defend them. Can they save this uncommon common?